FUELS DIET
COOKBOOK

AN ACCURATE SELECTION OF EASY, FLAVORFUL RECIPES FOR LIFELONG HEALTH

ANNALISA WILLIAMS

© Copyright 2021 by A. WILLIAMS - All rights reserved.

The following Book is reproduced below with the goal of providing information that is as accurate and reliable as possible.

Regardless, purchasing this Book can be seen as consent to the fact that both the publisher and the author of this book are in no way experts on the topics discussed within and that any recommendations or suggestions that are made herein are for entertainment purposes only.

Professionals should be consulted as needed prior to undertaking any of the action endorsed herein.

This declaration is deemed fair and valid by both the American Bar Association and the Committee of Publishers Association and is legally binding throughout the United States.

Furthermore, the transmission, duplication, or reproduction of any of the following work including specific information will be considered an illegal act irrespective of if it is done electronically or in print. This extends to creating a secondary or tertiary copy of the work or a recorded copy and is only allowed with the express written consent from the Publisher. All additional right reserved.

The information in the following pages is broadly considered a truthful and accurate account of facts and as such, any inattention, use, or misuse of the information in question by the reader will render any resulting actions solely under their purview.

There are no scenarios in which the publisher or the original author of this work can be in any fashion deemed liable for any hardship or damages that may befall them after undertaking information described herein.

Additionally, the information in the following pages is intended only for informational purposes and should thus be thought of as universal.

As befitting its nature, it is presented without assurance regarding its prolonged validity or interim quality.

<u>Trademarks that are mentioned are done without written consent and can in no way be considered an endorsement from the trademark holder.</u>

TABLE OF CONTENT

INTRODUCTION 8
WHAT FUELS DIET CONSIST OF? 13
HOW EASY IS TO FOLLOW FUELS DIET? 16
FOOD TO EAT AND FOOD TO AVOID 20
LEAN AND GREEN RECIPES 27
    BROCCOLI CHEDDAR BREAKFAST BAKE 29
    GRILLED MAHI MAHI WITH JICAMA SLAW 30
FUELS RECIPES 31
    AVOCADO SHRIMP CUCUMBER BITES 33
    CRISPY CAULIFLOWERS 34
    STRAWBERRY-AVOCADO TOAST WITH BALSAMIC GLAZE
    35
    RAW-CINNAMON-APPLE NUT BOWL 36
    PEANUT BUTTER AND CACAO BREAKFAST QUINOA 37
    SPICED PUMPKIN MUFFINS 38
BREAKFAST 41
    SHAKE CAKE FUELING 43
    BISCUIT PIZZA 44
    MINI MAC IN A BOWL 45
    QUINOA PORRIDGE 47
    AMARANTH PORRIDGE 48
    HEMP SEED PORRIDGE 49
    PUMPKIN SPICE QUINOA 50
MAINS 51
    HIGH PROTEIN CHICKEN MEATBALLS 53
    BARLEY RISOTTO 54
    BALSAMIC BEEF AND MUSHROOMS MIX 55
    OREGANO PORK MIX 56
    CUCUMBER BOWL WITH SPICES AND GREEK YOGURT 57
    STUFFED BELL PEPPERS WITH QUINOA 58
    GARLIC CHICKEN BALLS 60
SNACKS RECIPES 61

- VEGGIE FRITTERS 63
- WHITE BEAN DIP 64
- ZUCCHINI FRITTER 65
- CUCUMBER SANDWICH BITES 67
- OLIVES AND CHEESE STUFFED TOMATOES 68
- BACON CHEESEBURGER 69
- PERSONAL PIZZA BISCUIT 71
- GRANDMA'S RICE 72

VEGETABLES 75
- GREEN BEANS 77
- ASPARAGUS AVOCADO SOUP 78
- FENNEL AND ARUGULA SALAD WITH FIG VINAIGRETTE 80
- MIXED POTATO GRATIN 81
- HUMMUS 83

MEAT 85
- GRILLED CHICKEN POWER BOWL WITH GREEN GODDESS DRESSING 87
- TURKEY CAPRESE MEATLOAF CUPS 89
- AVOCADO CHICKEN SALAD 90

SOUPS AND STEWS 91
- ROASTED TOMATO SOUP 93
- CHEESEBURGER SOUP 94
- MUSHROOM & JALAPEÑO STEW 96

SMOOTHIES 99
- AVOCADO KALE SMOOTHIE 101
- APPLE KALE CUCUMBER SMOOTHIE 102
- STRAWBERRY MILKSHAKE 103
- CACTUS SMOOTHIE 104

DESSERTS 105
- DARK CHOCOLATE MOCHACCINO ICE BOMBS 107
- CHOCOLATE BARK WITH ALMONDS 108
- VANILLA BEAN FRAPPUCCINO 109
- SMOOTH PEANUT BUTTER CREAM 110
- VANILLA AVOCADO POPSICLES 111
- CHOCOLATE ALMOND BUTTER BROWNIE 112
- ALMOND BUTTER FUDGE 113

INTRODUCTION

Eating healthy food and doing regular physical activity are the 2 fundamental components for our health in general.
All existing diets, whether they are slimming or maintenance diets, are based on a selection of foods and ways of cooking compared to others and obviously they change according to our needs.
Nowadays when we decide to follow a slimming diet, we find ourselves in front of a wide range of choices because in the last few years many so many have been created, some of them aim to involve the subject in a drastic food change by subjecting him/her to hours of fasting.
So the subject in question prey to a momentary emotional attack lets himself be washed by a diet coach or a commercial rather than a new recipe book and decides to start his journey towards weight loss full of good proposals.

How long will it last?

The real problem is right here ...

One of the most common errors of the newcomers is to choose a diet too complicated to follow or that does not fit their lifestyle, and maybe after the sprint of 2 days will end up abandoning diet and coach and return to the previous diet more hungry than before.

Based on my decades of experience in the field, I can say that dieting with the intent to maintain a certain diet for longer or shorter periods until the

achievement of a goal is not as simple as many believe...
I personally believe that to get an 80% probability of succeeding in reaching the set objectives with a diet, it is necessary to compare the path to the construction of a house, metaphorically speaking.

For the construction of any building solid and durable over time, you must first dig a big hole, then build the foundation and only after these 2 steps you can apply some design.
The same thing must happen to us when we decide to go on a diet.

Even before you decide which diet to follow, it is necessary, in my opinion, to "start digging"!
Dig inside yourself:
What are the reasons why you want to lose weight?
Are these reasons really worth the effort?
Would you really be able to achieve this goal?
But more importantly...
What technique are you going to use to keep the winning mindset?
Yes, looking inside yourself and triggering the right emotions is the exercise that I believe is fundamental for the success of any diet because our mind is the basis of everything.
How strong is your why?
I can assure you that for the success of this exercise you do not need any coach, because the only person who can touch the bottom of your soul with the fingers is only you ...
My advice for dealing with this first phase is to dedicate 10 minutes a day (or even more than 10 minutes when you have taken the practice with the exercise) to talk to your soul.

I do not want you to misinterpret this book as a yoga course... It's actually very simple,
I am not asking you to learn the Yoga techniques of Tibetan monks, what I am asking you to do is to approach meditation practices.
I personally like very much to meditate early in the morning, maybe on the beach with the the sound of waves and seagulls singing, or in the middle of a green field or simply on the floor of my living room, any place that offers me 30 minutes of silence.
All you need to do is sit comfortably, close your eyes or look at a fixed point and begin to clear your mind. Do not focus on the breath, just take long breaths but focus on yourself for 10 minutes try to look inside yourself analyzing what are your weaknesses and touch them with your hands ....
Nothing more, it requires no special technique, only these simple actions applied for a minimum of 10 minutes a day, with consistency, honesty and without fear of looking inside.
Initially you may not feel at ease, but I assure you that after a couple of weeks you will became addicted to this exercise.
When you decide to embark on a diet, you must face the fact that it involves a change in your lifestyle, especially in your daily habits.
After this emotional journey we start to structure our diet according to our goals or needs, trying to identify (perhaps with the help of an expert) which is the method that best suits us by going to marry our rhythm of life.

Never forget that a healthy diet must be above all balanced, as our body needs carbohydrates, proteins, fats, fibres and vitamins to function properly.
body needs carbohydrates, proteins, fats, fibres and vitamins to function properly,

none of these 5 substances should be eliminated but all should be contained in each meal in a proportionate manner.
Almost as important as the first phase is the daily maintenance of a certain lifestyle for a certain period; After a couple of weeks in general people begin to feel some weaknesses, allow yourself a little break the rules (maybe once a week) it is worth of our psyche, the important thing is never losing sight of the goal.
When you have managed to shape your new lifestyle on the basis of a healthy diet alternating with regular physical activity you will not even realize that you have finally managed to lose those damn unwanted pounds!
Now they are just a bad memory...
At this point you can begin the third phase:
"Beautifying your body by working the muscle mass in the areas that most need to be toned".
I hope this small summary of my decades of experience in the field can give you some clarity and I hope you will be able to find your balance by following my recipes.

WHAT FUELS DIET CONSIST OF?

The Fuel diet is a Practice that aims to reduce or maintain current weight. It is a diet that recommends eating a combination of Processed foods called fuels and home-cooked meals (lean and green meals).

It is believed that it sticks to the brand Product (input) and supplements it with meat, vegetables, and fatty snacks; this will keep you satisfied and nourished. At the same time you don't need to worry much about losing muscles because you are eating enough Protein and consuming too few calories. And that way, the individual who Practices the diet can lose around 12 Pounds in just 12 weeks using the ideal 5&1 weight Plan.

In short, the fuels diet is a Program that focuses on cutting calories and reducing carbohydrates in meals. To do this effectively, combine Packaged foods called "fuels" with home-cooked meals, which encourages weight loss.

Like many commercial Plans, Fuels diet involves buying most of the foods Permitted on a diet in Packaged form. The company deals on a wide range of food Products that they call "fuels"—on its website.

These include Pancakes, shakes, Pasta dishes, soups, cookies, mashed Potatoes, and Popcorn.

Users Pick the Plan that best suits them. The 5 & 1 Plan entails eating five small meals Per day. The meals can be selected from more than 60 substitutable fuels, including one "lean and green" meal, Probably veggies or protein that you will Prepare by yourself.

HOW EASY IS TO FOLLOW FUELS DIET?

Practicing the Fuels diet gives you an option of about 60 Fuels, but that is not to say you will still not have yearnings for other food options, especially those you are used to before taking up the diet Plan.

All the recipes are readily available, and you can also take the option of dining out by following your guide. However, alcohol consumption is Prohibited. You can order your
meals easily or prepare them in your kitchen under a few minutes. You can easily get the needed tools to make your meals from your coach or request for help on the online community.
You can get various ideas for your lean and green meals by visiting the brand Pinterest Page. You will also get a recipe conversion guide that you can use whenever you have
trouble with your recipe measurement.
You might face many challenges whenever you decide to eat out. However, it is not impossible to eat out. To be on the safe side, the brand advised you to let your Lean and Green meals be the only option when you consider eating out. By going through the dining out guide, you will get the clue on how to navigate buffets, order beverages, and selecting condiments and toppings for your meals.
It is straightforward to choose a Plan and make your order that will be delivered instantly. Food Preparation is swift, and the only area where you can face difficulty is adding water and nuking in the microwave. Anyone with no knowledge of cooking can

easily tackle and get over the Preparation of Preparing the meals without breaking a sweat.

The Fuels coaches aim to help you adopt healthy habits. You will get weekly, and monthly support calls from the Fuels coaches. Once you are a member of the community, you will also be able to Partake in community events and have access to the nutrition support team, mainly composed of dietitians.

Informational guides and FAQs can also be accessed online easily and for free.

The company says the recommended meals have a high "fullness index," which means that the high Protein and fiber contents in the meals should help get full for an extended Period.

The meals you will be taking are tailored for the weight and fat loss Purpose and may not likely win a cuisine competition. It is Pertinent to note that the Fuels you will feed on will not contain flavors, artificial colors, or sweeteners.

No matter the Plan you Pick out, you start by using having a smartphone communique with a tutor to help determine which Fuels Plan to follow, set weight loss desires, and make yourself familiar with the application.

Eating out can be challenging, but still Possible. If you love eating out, you can download Fuels dining out guide. The guide comes with tips on how to navigate buffets, order beverages, and choose condiments. Aside from following the guide, you can also ask the chef to make substitutions for the ingredients used in cooking your food. For instance, you can ask the chef to serve no more than 7 ounces of steak and serve it with steamed broccoli instead of baked Potatoes.

opt for lean and green foods that have high fullness index. Eat foods that contain high Protein and fiber content as they can keep you full for longer periods. In fact, many nutrition experts highlight the importance of satiety when it comes to weight loss.

You have access to knowledgeable coaches. If you follow the Fuels Diet Plan, you have access to knowledgeable coaches and become a Part of a community that will give you access to support calls and community events. You also have a standby nutrition support team that can answer your questions.

Irrespective of the diet Plan you Pick, you commence by having a teleconference with a certain coach to assist in determining which Fuels diet Plan to follow, established weight loss objectives, and acquaint yourself with the Platform.

How Much Does Fuels diet Cost?

In comparison, the United States Department of Agriculture estimates that a woman whose ages range from 10-50 can follow a nutritious diet while spending as little as $166.40 Per month on groceries. As long as she is Preparing all her meals at home.

FOOD TO EAT AND FOOD TO AVOID

There are a lot many foods that you can eat while following the Fuels Diet. However, you must know these foods by heart. This is Particularly true if you are just new to this diet, and you have to follow the 5&1 Fuels Diet Plan strictly. Thus, this section is dedicated to the types of foods that are recommended and those to avoid while following this diet regimen.

FOOD TO EAT

There are numerous categories of foods that can be eaten under this diet regimen. This section will break down the Lean and Green foods that you can eat while following this diet regime.

LEAN FOOD

Leanest Foods - These foods are considered to be the leanest as it has only up to 4 grams of total fat. Moreover, dieters should eat a 7-ounce cooked Portion of these foods. Consume these foods with 1 healthy fat serving.
- Fish: Flounder, cod, haddock, grouper, Mahi, tilapia, tuna (yellowfin fresh or canned), and wild catfish.
- Shellfish: Scallops, lobster, crabs, shrimp
- Game meat: Elk, deer, buffalo
- Ground turkey or other meat: Should be 98% lean

- Meatless alternatives: 14 egg whites, 2 cups egg substitute, 5 ounces seitan, 1 ½ Cups 1% cottage cheese, and 12 ounces non-fat 0% Greek yogurt

Leaner Foods - These foods contain 5 to 9 grams of total fat. Consume these foods with 1 healthy fat serving. Make sure to consume only 6 ounces of a cooked Portion of these foods daily:
- Fish: Halibut, trout, and swordfish
- Chicken: White meat such as breasts as long as the skin is removed
- Turkey: Ground turkey as long as it is 95% to 97% lean.
- Meatless oPtions: 2 whole eggs Plus 4 egg whites, 2 whole eggs Plus one cup egg substitute, 1 ½ Cups 2% cottage cheese, and 12 ounces low fat 2% Plain Greek yogurt

Lean Foods - These are foods that contain 10g to 20g total fat. When consuming these foods, there should be no serving of healthy fat. These include the following:
- Fish: Tuna (bluefin steak), salmon, herring, farmed catfish, and mackerel
- Lean beef: Ground, steak, and roast
- Lamb: All cuts
- Pork: Pork chops, Pork tenderloin, and all Parts. Make sure to remove the skin
- Ground turkey and other meats: 85% to 94% lean
- Chicken: Any dark meat
- Meatless oPtions: 15 ounces extra-firm tofu, 3 whole eggs (uP to two times Per week), 4 ounces reduced-fat skim cheese, 8 ounces Part-skim ricotta cheese, and 5 ounces tempeh

Healthy Fat Servings - Healthy fat servings are allowed under this diet. They should contain 5 grams of fat and less than grams of carbohydrates.

Regardless of what type of Fuels Diet Plan you follow, make sure that you add between 0 and 2 healthy fat servings daily. Below are the different healthy fat servings that you can eat:
- 1 Teaspoon oil (any kind of oil)
- 1 Tablespoon low carbohydrate salad dressing
- 2 Tablespoons reduced-fat salad dressing
- 5 to 10 black or green olives
- 1 ½ ounce avocado
- 1/3-ounce Plain nuts including peanuts, almonds, Pistachios
- 1 Tablespoon Plain seeds such as chia, sesame, flax, and Pumpkin seeds
- ½ Tablespoon regular butter, mayonnaise, and margarine

GREEN FOOD

This section will discuss the green servings that you still need to consume while following the Fuels Diet Plan. These include all kinds of vegetables that have been categorized from lower, moderate, and high in terms of carbohydrate content. One serving of vegetables should be at ½ cup unless otherwise specified.

Lower Carbohydrate - These are vegetables that contain low amounts of carbohydrates. If you are following the 5&1 Fuels Diet Plan, then these vegetables are good for you.

- A cup of green leafy vegetables, such as collard greens (raw), lettuce (green leaf, iceberg, butterhead, and romaine), spinach (raw), mustard greens, spring mix, bok choy (raw), and watercress.

- ½ cup of vegetables including cucumbers, celery, radishes, white mushroom, sprouts (mung bean, alfalfa), arugula, turnip greens, escarole, noPales, Swiss chard (raw), Jalapeno, and bok choy (cooked).

Moderate Carbohydrate - These are vegetables that contain moderate amounts of carbohydrates. Below are the types of vegetables that can be consumed in moderation:

- ½ cup of any of the following vegetables such as asparagus, cauliflower, fennel bulb, eggplant, Portabella mushrooms, kale, cooked spinach, summer squash (zucchini and scallop).

Higher Carbohydrates - Foods that are under this category contain a high amount of starch. Make sure to consume limited amounts of these vegetables.
- ½ cup of the following vegetables like chayote squash, red cabbage, broccoli, cooked collard and mustard greens, green or wax beans, kohlrabi, kabocha squash, cooked leeks, any Peppers, okra, raw scallion, summer squash such as straight neck and crookneck, tomatoes, Spaghetti squash, turnips, jicama, cooked Swiss chard, and hearts of Palm.

FOOD TO AVOID

With the exclusion of carbohydrates in the Prepackaged Fuels, most carbohydrate containing beverages foods and are forbidden while doing the 5&1 diet Plan. Certain fats are also not allowed, as well as all fried foods because they are high in saturated fats.
There are many types of foods that are not allowed for the Fuels Diet Plan. These
foods either contain high amounts of fats or carbohydrates that can contribute to weight gain. Below are the types of foods that are not allowed under this Particular diet—unless included in the Fuels.

- Generous Desserts

Unsurprisingly, Fuels dejects spoiling your sugar desires with sweets like ice cream, cakes, cookies and the likes.

Nevertheless, after the Preliminary weight loss Phase, reasonable sweet indulgences like freshly Picked fruits or sweetened yogurt can be allowed their way back to your strict Fuels diet.

- High Caloric Additions

Shortening, butter and elevated fat salad dressings increases flavor; however, they also increase large sums of calories. On Fuels, you will be advised to keep add-ons to a minimum or substitute lesser calorie forms.

- Alcohol

The Fuels diet boosts customers to minimize alcohol consumption. If you are trying to stay within a stern calorie range, a 5-ounce glass of beer for 120 calories or the 150 calories in a 12-ounce glass of wine will add up fast.

- Fried and High-Fat Foods Additionally, you cannot eat:

- Certain fats: butter, coconut oil, solid shortening.

- Whole fat dairy: milk, cheese, yogurt.

- Sugar-sweetened beverages: soda, fruit juice, sports drinks, energy drinks, sweet tea.

- Food allowed in the Maintenance Plan

The following foods will not be allowed while on the 5&1 Plan but added back through the 6-week transition Phase and allowed during the 3&3 Plan:

- Fruit: all fresh fruit.

- Low in fat or fat-free dairy Products: milk, cheese, yogurt.

- Total grains: total grain bread, high roughage breakfast cereal, brown or black or red rice, total wheat Pasta.

- Legumes: lentils, soybeans, Peas, beans.

LEAN AND GREEN RECIPES

BROCCOLI CHEDDAR BREAKFAST BAKE

COOKING: 45' PREPARATION: 10' SERVES: 4

INGREDIENTS

- 9 eggs
- 6 cups of small broccoli florets
- ¼ teaspoon of salt
- 1 cup of unsweetened almond milk
- ¼ teaspoon of cayenne pepper
- ¼ teaspoon of ground pepper
- Cooking spray
- 4 oz. of shredded, reduced-fat cheddar

DIRECTIONS

1. Preheat your oven to about 375 degrees
2. In your large microwave-safe, add broccoli and 2 to 3 tablespoon of water. Microwave on high heat for 4 minutes or until it becomes tender. Now transfer the broccoli to a colander to drain excess liquid
3. Get a medium-sized bowl and whisk the milk, eggs, and seasonings together.
4. Set the broccoli neatly on the bottom of a lightly greased 13 x 9-inch baking dish. Sprinkle the cheese gently on the broccoli and pour the egg mixture on top of it.
5. Bake for about 45 minutes or until the center is set and the top forms a light brown crust.

NUTRITIONS: Calories: 290 Protein: 25g Carbohydrate: 8g Fat: 18 g

GRILLED MAHI MAHI WITH JICAMA SLAW

COOKING: 20' PREPARATION: 10' SERVES: 4

INGREDIENTS

- 1 teaspoon each for pepper and salt, divided
- 1 tablespoon of lime juice, divided
- 2 tablespoon + 2 teaspoons of extra virgin oil
- 4 raw mahi-mahi fillets, which should be 8 oz
- ½ cucumber which should be thinly cut into long strips like matchsticks (it should yield about 1 cup)
- 1 jicama, which should be thinly cut into long strips like matchsticks (it should yield about 3 cups)
- 1 cup of alfalfa sprouts
- 2 cups of coarsely chopped watercress

DIRECTIONS

1. Combine ½ teaspoon of both pepper and salt, 1 tea-spoon of lime juice, and 2 teaspoons of oil in a small bowl. Then brush the mahi-mahi fillets all through with the olive oil mixture.
2. Grill the mahi-mahi on medium-high heat until it becomes done in about 5 minutes, turn it to the other side, and let it be done for about 5 minutes. (You will have an internal temperature of about 1450F).
3. For the slaw, combine the watercress, cucumber, jicama, and alfalfa sprouts in a bowl. Now combine ½ teaspoon of both pepper and salt, 2 teaspoons of lime juice, and 2 tablespoons of extra virgin oil in a small bowl. Drizzle it over slaw and toss together to combine.

NUTRITIONS: Calories:320 Protein:44g Carbohydrate:10g Fat: 11g

FUELS RECIPES

AVOCADO SHRIMP CUCUMBER BITES

COOKING: 10' PREPARATION: 10' SERVES: 6

INGREDIENTS

» 1 large cucumber, cut into thick circles
» 6 small shrimp
» 1/2 cup parmesan cheese, grated
» 1 tsp. almond butter, cubed
» Salt and pepper to taste
» 1 tsp. coriander, chopped

DIRECTIONS

1. Preheat the oven to 390 degrees F.
2. Add wax paper on a baking sheet.
3. Arrange the cucumber pieces on the baking sheet.
4. Add one shrimp on each slice.
5. Add the butter cubes, cheese, salt, pepper, and coriander on top.
6. Bake for 10 minutes. Serve.

NUTRITIONS: Fat: 2g Cholesterol: 51 mg Sodium: 240 mg Potassium: 83 mg Carbohydrates: 1 g Protein: 4 g

CRISPY CAULIFLOWERS

COOKING: 10' PREPARATION: 10' SERVES: 4

INGREDIENTS

- 2 cup cauliflower florets, diced
- 1/2 cup almond flour
- 1/2 cup coconut flour
- Salt and pepper to taste
- 1 tsp. mixed herbs
- 1 tsp. chives, chopped
- 1 egg
- 1 tsp. cumin
- 1/2 tsp. garlic powder
- 1 cup water
- Oil for frying

DIRECTIONS

1. Combine the egg, salt, garlic, water, cumin, chives, mixed herbs, pepper, and flour in a mixing bowl.
2. Add the cauliflower in the mixture and then fry them in oil until they become golden in color.
3. Serve.

NUTRITIONS: Protein: 3.3 g Carbohydrates: 19.4 g Fiber: 1.3 g Fat: 10.4 g

STRAWBERRY-AVOCADO TOAST WITH BALSAMIC GLAZE

COOKING: 30'   PREPARATION: 5' SERVES: 4

INGREDIENTS

- » 1 avocado, peeled, pitted, and quartered
- » 4 whole-wheat bread slices, toasted
- » 4 ripe strawberries, cut into 1/4-inch slices
- » 1 tablespoon balsamic glaze or reduction

DIRECTIONS

1. Mash one-quarter of the avocado on a slice of toast.
2. Layer one-quarter of the strawberry slices over the avocado, and finish with a drizzle of balsamic glaze.
3. Repeat with the remaining ingredients and serve.
4. Tip: If you can't buy balsamic glaze, make your own! Put balsamic vinegar in a small saucepan and cook, uncovered, over low heat for roughly 45 minutes, or until it's reduced to nearly one-quarter of the original amount of liquid.

NUTRITIONS: Fat: 8 g Carbohydrates: 17 g Fiber: 5 g Protein: 5 g

RAW-CINNAMON-APPLE NUT BOWL

COOKING: 1H TO CHILL PREPARATION: 15' SERVES:1

INGREDIENTS

- One green apple halved, seeded, and cored
- 3/4 Honey crisp apples, halved, seeded, cored
- 1/4 teaspoon freshly squeezed lemon juice
- One pitted Medrol dates
- 1/8 teaspoon ground cinnamon
- Pinch ground nutmeg
- 1/2 tablespoons chia seeds, plus more for serving (optional)
- 1/4 tablespoon hemp seed
- 1/8 cup chopped walnuts
- Nut butter, for serving (optional)

DIRECTIONS

1. Finely dice half the green apple and 1 Honey crisp apple. With the lemon juice, store it in an airtight container while you work on the next steps.
2. Coarsely chop the remaining apples and the dates. Transfer to a food processor and add the cinnamon and nutmeg. Check it several times if it combines, then processes for 2 to 3 minutes to puree. Stir the puree into the reserved diced apples. Stir in the chia seeds (if using), hemp seeds, and walnuts. Chill for at least 1 hour. Enjoy!
3. Serve as is or top with additional chia seeds and nut butter (if using).

NUTRITIONS: Calories: 274 Fat: 8g Protein: 4g Carbohydrates: 52g Fiber: 9g

PEANUT BUTTER AND CACAO BREAKFAST QUINOA

COOKING: 10' PREPARATION: 10' SERVES: 1

INGREDIENTS

- 1/3 cup quinoa flakes
- 1/2 cup unsweetened nondairy milk,
- 1/2 cup of water
- 1/8 cup raw cacao powder
- One tablespoon natural creamy peanut butter
- 1/8 teaspoon ground cinnamon
- One banana, mashed
- Fresh berries of choice, for serving
- Chopped nuts of choice, for serving

DIRECTIONS

1. Using an 8-quart pot over medium-high heat, stir together the quinoa flakes, milk, water, cacao pow- der, peanut butter, and cinnamon. Cook and stir it until the mixture begins to simmer. Turn the heat to medium-low and cook for 3 to 5 minutes, stirring frequently.
2. Stir in the bananas and cook until hot.
3. Serve topped with fresh berries, nuts, and a splash of milk.

NUTRITIONS: Calories: 471 Fat: 16 g Carbohydrates: 69g Fiber: 18 g Protein: 18 g

SPICED PUMPKIN MUFFINS

COOKING: 20' PREPARATION: 15' SERVES: 1

INGREDIENTS

- 1/6 tablespoons ground flaxseed
- 1/24 cup of water
- 1/8 cups whole wheat flour
- 1/6 teaspoons baking powder
- 5/6 teaspoons ground cinnamon
- 1/12 teaspoon baking soda
- 1/12 teaspoon ground ginger
- 1/16 teaspoon ground nutmeg
- 1/32 teaspoon ground cloves
- 1/6 cup pumpkin puree
- 1/12 cup pure maple syrup
- 1/24 cup unsweetened applesauce
- 1/24 cup unsweetened nondairy milk
- 1/2 teaspoons vanilla extract

DIRECTIONS

1. Preheat the oven to 350°F. Line a 12-cup metal muffin pan with parchment paper liners or use a silicone muffin pan.
2. First, mix the flaxseed and water in a large bowl then keep it aside.
3. In a medium bowl, stir together the flour, baking powder, cinnamon, baking soda, ginger, nutmeg, and cloves.
4. In a medium bowl, stir up the maple syrup, pumpkin puree, applesauce, milk, and vanilla. Crease

the wet ingredients into the dry ingredients make use of a spatula.
5. Fold the soaked flaxseed into the batter until evenly combined, but do not over mix the batter, or your muffins will become dense. Spoon about 1/4 cup of batter per muffin into your prepared muffin pan.
6. Bake for 18 to 20 minutes, or until a toothpick inserted into the center of a muffin comes out clean. Remove the muffins from the pan.
7. Transfer to a wire rack for cooling.
8. Store in an airtight container that is at room temperature.

NUTRITIONS: Calories: 115 Fat: 1g Protein: 3g Carbohydrates: 25g Fiber: 3g

BREAKFAST

SHAKE CAKE FUELING

COOKING: 0 PREPARATION: 2' SERVES: 1

INGREDIENTS

» One packet of shakes.
» 1/4 teaspoon of baking powder
» Two tablespoons of eggbeaters or egg whites
» Two tablespoons of water
» Other options that are not compulsory include sweetener, reduced-fat cream cheese, etc.

DIRECTIONS
1. Begin by preheating the oven.

2. Mix all the ingredients begin with the dry ingredients first before adding the wet ingredients.
3. After the mixture/batter is ready, pour gently into muffin cups.
4. Inside the oven, place, and bake for about 16-18minutes or until it is baked and ready. Allow it to cool completely.
5. Add additional toppings of your choice and ensure your delicious shake cake is refreshing.

NUTRITIONS: Calories: 896 Fat: 37 g Carbohydrate: 115 g Protein: 34 g

BISCUIT PIZZA

COOKING: 15' PREPARATION: 20' SERVES: 1

INGREDIENTS

» 1/4 sachet of buttermilk cheddar and herb biscuit
» 1/4 tablespoon of tomato sauce
» 1/4 tablespoon of low-fat shredded cheese
» 1/4 table of water
» Parchment paper

DIRECTIONS

1. You may begin by preheating the oven to about 350°F
2. Mix the biscuit and water and stir properly.
3. In the parchment paper, pour the mixture and spread it into a thin circle. Allow cooking for 10 minutes.
4. Take it out and add the tomato sauce and shredded cheese.
5. Bake it for a few more minutes.

NUTRITIONS: Calories: 121 Fat: 12 g Carbohydrate: 45 g Protein: 12 g

MINI MAC IN A BOWL

COOKING: 15' PREPARATION: 5' SERVES: 1

INGREDIENTS

- 5 ounce of lean ground beef
- Two tablespoons of diced white or yellow onion.
- 1/8 teaspoon of onion powder
- 1/8 teaspoon of white vinegar
- 1 ounce of dill pickle slices
- One teaspoon sesame seed
- 3 cups of shredded Romaine lettuce
- Cooking spray
- Two tablespoons reduced-fat shredded cheddar cheese
- Two tablespoons of Wish-bone light thousand island as dressing

DIRECTIONS

1. Place a lightly greased small skillet on fire to heat,
2. Add your onion to cook for about 2-3 minutes,
3. Next, add the beef and allow cooking until it's brown
4. Next, mix your vinegar and onion powder with the dressing,
5. Finally, top the lettuce with the cooked meat and sprinkle cheese on it, add your pickle slices.
6. Drizzle the mixture with the sauce and sprinkle the sesame seeds also.

7.   Your mini mac in a bowl is ready for consumption.

NUTRITIONS: Calories: 150 Protein: 21 g Carbohydrates: 32 g Fats: 19 g

QUINOA PORRIDGE

COOKING: 25' PREPARATION: 5' SERVES: 2

INGREDIENTS

- 2 cups coconut milk
- 1 cup rinsed quinoa
- 1/8 tsp. ground cinnamon
- 1 cup fresh blueberries

DIRECTIONS

1. In a saucepan, boil the coconut milk over high heat.
2. Add the quinoa to the milk then bring the mixture to a boil.
3. You then let it simmer for 15 minutes on medium heat until the milk is reduces.
4. Add the cinnamon then mix it properly in the sauce- pan.
5. Cover the saucepan and cook for at least 8 minutes until milk is completely absorbed.
6. Add in the blueberries then cook for 30 more sec- onds.
7. Serve.

NUTRITIONS: Calories: 271 kcal Fat: 3.7g Carbs: 54g Protein:6.5g

AMARANTH PORRIDGE

COOKING: 30' PREPARATION: 5' SERVES: 2

INGREDIENTS

- 2 cups coconut milk
- 2 cups alkaline water
- 1 cup amaranth
- 2 tbsps. coconut oil
- 1 tbsp. ground cinnamon

DIRECTIONS

1. In a saucepan, mix in the milk with water then boil the mixture.
2. You stir in the amaranth then reduce the heat to medium.
3. Cook on the medium heat then simmer for at least 30 minutes as you stir it occasionally.
4. Turn off the heat.
5. Add in cinnamon and coconut oil then stir.
6. Serve.

NUTRITIONS: Calories: 434 kcal Fat: 35g Carbs: 27g Protein: 6.7g

HEMP SEED PORRIDGE

COOKING: 5' PREPARATION: 5' SERVES: 6

INGREDIENTS

- 3 cups cooked hemp seed
- 1 packet Stevia
- 1 cup coconut milk

DIRECTIONS

1. In a saucepan, mix the rice and the coconut milk over moderate heat for about 5 minutes as you stir it constantly.
2. Remove the pan from the burner then add the Ste- via. Stir.
3. Serve in 6 bowls.
4. Enjoy.

NUTRITIONS: Calories: 236 kcal Fat: 1.8g Carbs: 48.3g Protein: 7g

PUMPKIN SPICE QUINOA

COOKING: 0' PREPARATION: 10' SERVES: 2

INGREDIENTS

- 1 cup cooked quinoa
- 1 cup unsweetened coconut milk
- 1 large mashed banana
- 1/4 cup pumpkin puree
- 1 tsp. pumpkin spice
- 2 tsps. chia seeds

DIRECTIONS

1. In a container, mix all the ingredients.
2. Seal the lid then shake the container properly to mix.
3. Refrigerate overnight.
4. Serve.

NUTRITIONS: Calories: 212 kcal Fat: 11.9g Carbs: 31.7g Protein: 7.3g

MAINS

HIGH PROTEIN CHICKEN MEATBALLS

COOKING: 25' PREPARATION: 5' SERVES: 2

INGREDIENTS

- Chicken (1 lbs., lean, ground)
- Oats (3/4 cup, rolled)
- Onions (2, grated)
- All spice (2 tsp. ground)
- Salt and black pepper (dash)

DIRECTIONS

1. Heat a skillet (large) over medium heat then grease
using cooking spray.
2. Add in the onions (grated), chicken (lean, ground), oats (rolled), allspice (earth) and a dash of salt and black pepper in in a large sized bowl, stir well to incorporate.
3. Shape mixture into meatballs (small).
4. Place into the skillet (greased). Cook for roughly 5
minutes until golden brown on all sides.
5. Remove meatballs from heat then serve immediate- ly.

NUTRITIONS: Calories: 519 Cal Protein: 57g
Carbohydrates: 32 g Fat :15 g

BARLEY RISOTTO

COOKING: 7-8H PREPARATION: 15' SERVES: 8

INGREDIENTS

- 2 1/4 cups hulled barley, rinsed
- 1 onion, finely chopped
- 4 garlic cloves, minced
- 1 (8-ounce) package button mushrooms, chopped
- 6 cups low-sodium vegetable broth
- 1/2 teaspoon dried marjoram leaves
- 1/8 teaspoon freshly ground black pepper
- 2/3 cup grated Parmesan cheese

DIRECTIONS

1. In a 6-quart slow cooker, mix the barley, onion, garlic, mushrooms, broth, marjoram, and pepper.
2. Cover and cook on low for 7 to 8 hours, or until the barley has absorbed most of the liquid and is tender, and the vegetables are tender.
3. Stir in the Parmesan cheese and serve.

NUTRITIONS: Calories: 288 Cal Carbohydrates: 45 g Sugar: 2 g Fiber: 9 g Fat: 6 g Saturated Fat: 3 g Protein: 13 g Sodium: 495 mg

BALSAMIC BEEF AND MUSHROOMS MIX

COOKING: 8H PREPARATION: 5' SERVES: 4

INGREDIENTS

- 2 pounds' beef, cut into strips
- ¼ cup balsamic vinegar
- 2 cups beef stock
- 1 tablespoon ginger, grated
- Juice of ½ lemon
- 1 cup brown mushrooms, sliced
- A pinch of salt and black pepper
- 1 teaspoon ground cinnamon

DIRECTIONS

1. In your slow cooker, mix all the ingredients, cover and cook on low for 8 hours.
2. Divide everything between plates and serve.

NUTRITIONS: Calories: 446 Fat: 14g Fiber: 0.6g Carbs: 2.9 g Protein: 70g

OREGANO PORK MIX

COOKING: 7H 6' PREPARATION: 5' SERVES: 4

INGREDIENTS

- 2 pounds' pork roast
- 7 ounces' tomato paste
- 1 yellow onion, chopped
- 1 cup beef stock
- 2 tablespoons ground cumin
- 2 tablespoons olive oil
- 2 tablespoons fresh oregano, chopped
- 1 tablespoon garlic, minced
- ½ cup fresh thyme, chopped

DIRECTIONS

1. Heat up a sauté pan with the oil over medium-high heat, add the roast, brown it for 3 minutes on both side and then transfer to your slow cooker.
2. Add the remaining ingredients, toss a bit, cover and
cook on low for 7 hours.
3. Slice the roast, divide it between plates and serve.

NUTRITIONS: Calories: 623 Fat: 30.1g Fiber: 6.2g Carbs: 19.3g Protein: 69.2g

CUCUMBER BOWL WITH SPICES AND GREEK YOGURT

COOKING: 20' PREPARATION: 10' SERVES: 3

INGREDIENTS

- 4 cucumbers
- ½ teaspoon chili pepper
- ¼ cup fresh parsley, chopped
- ¾ cup fresh dill, chopped
- 2 tablespoons lemon juice
- ½ teaspoon salt
- ½ teaspoon ground black pepper
- ¼ teaspoon sage
- ½ teaspoon dried oregano
- 1/3 cup Greek yogurt

DIRECTIONS

1. Make the cucumber dressing: blend the dill and parsley until you get green mash.
2. Then combine together green mash with lemon juice, salt, ground black pepper, sage, dried oregano, Greek yogurt, and chili pepper.
3. Churn the mixture well.
4. Chop the cucumbers roughly and combine them with cucumber dressing. Mix up well.
5. Refrigerate the cucumber for 20 minutes.

NUTRITIONS: Calories: 114 Fat: 1.6g Fiber: 4.1g Carbs: 23.2g Protein: 7.6g

STUFFED BELL PEPPERS WITH QUINOA

COOKING: 35' PREPARATION: 10' SERVES: 2

INGREDIENTS

- 2 bell peppers
- 1/3 cup quinoa
- 3 oz. chicken stock
- ¼ cup onion, diced
- ½ teaspoon salt
- ¼ teaspoon tomato paste
- ½ teaspoon dried oregano
- 1/3 cup sour cream
- 1 teaspoon paprika

DIRECTIONS

1. Trim the peppers and remove the seeds.
2. Then combine together chicken stock and quinoa in the pan.
3. Add salt and boil the ingredients for 10 minutes or
until quinoa will soak all liquid.
4. Then combine together cooked quinoa with dried oregano, tomato paste, and onion.
5. Fill the bell peppers with the quinoa mixture and arrange in the casserole mold.
6. Add sour cream and bake the peppers for 25 minutes
at 365F.
7. Serve the cooked peppers with sour cream sauce
from the casserole mold.

NUTRITIONS: Calories: 237 Fat: 10.3g Fiber: 4.1g Carbs: 31g Protein: 7g

GARLIC CHICKEN BALLS

COOKING: 10' PREPARATION: 15' SERVES: 4

INGREDIENTS

- 2 cups ground chicken
- 1 teaspoon minced garlic
- 1 teaspoon dried dill
- 1/3 carrot, grated
- 1 egg, beaten
- 1 tablespoon olive oil
- ¼ cup coconut flakes
- ½ teaspoon salt

DIRECTIONS

1. In the mixing bowl mix up together ground chicken, minced garlic, dried dill, carrot, egg, and salt.
2. Stir the chicken mixture with the help of the finger- tips until homogeneous.
3. Then make medium balls from the mixture.
4. Coat every chicken ball in coconut flakes.
5. Heat up olive oil in the skillet.
6. Add chicken balls and cook them for 3 minutes from each side. The cooked chicken balls will have a golden brown color.

NUTRITIONS: Calories: 200 Fat: 10.3g Fiber: 0.6g Carbs: 1.7g Protein: 2

SNACKS RECIPES

VEGGIE FRITTERS

COOKING: 10' PREPARATION: 10' SERVES: 4

INGREDIENTS

- 2 garlic cloves, minced
- 2 yellow onions, chopped
- 4 scallions, chopped
- 2 carrots, grated
- 2 teaspoons cumin, ground
- ½ teaspoon turmeric powder
- Salt and black pepper to the taste
- ¼ teaspoon coriander, ground
- 2 tablespoons parsley, chopped
- ¼ teaspoon lemon juice
- ½ cup almond flour
- 2 beets, peeled and grated
- 2 eggs, whisked
- ¼ cup tapioca flour
- 3 tablespoons olive oil

DIRECTIONS

1. In a bowl, combine the garlic with the onions, scallions and the rest of the ingredients except the oil, stir well and shape medium fritters out of this mix.
2. Heat oil in a pan over medium-high heat, add the fritters, cook for 5 minutes on each side, arrange on a platter and serve.

NUTRITIONS: Calories 209 Fat 11.2 g Fiber 3 g Carbs 4.4 g Protein 4.8 g

WHITE BEAN DIP

COOKING: 0' PREPARATION: 10' SERVES: 4

INGREDIENTS

- 15 ounces canned white beans, drained and rinsed
- 6 ounces canned artichoke hearts, drained and quartered
- 4 garlic cloves, minced
- 1 tablespoon basil, chopped
- 2 tablespoons olive oil
- Juice of ½ lemon
- Zest of ½ lemon, grated
- Salt and black pepper to the taste

DIRECTIONS

1. In your food processor, combine the beans with the artichokes and the rest of the ingredients except the oil and pulse well.
2. Add the oil gradually, pulse the mix again, divide into cups and serve as a party dip.

NUTRITIONS: Calories 274 Fat 11.7 g Fiber 6.5 g Carbs 18.5 g Protein 16.5 g

ZUCCHINI FRITTER

COOKING: 10' PREPARATION: 15' SERVES: 4

INGREDIENTS

- 1 1/2 pound of grated zucchini
- 1 Tsp. of salt
- 1/4 cup of grated Parmesan
- 1/4 cup of flour
- 2 cloves of minced garlic
- 2 Tbsp of olive oil
- 1 large egg
- Freshly ground black pepper and kosher salt to taste

DIRECTIONS

1. Put the grated zucchini into a colander over the sink
2. Add your salt and toss it to mix properly, then leave it to settle for about 10 minutes.
3. Next, use a clean cheese cloth to drain the zucchini completely.
4. Combine drained zucchini, Parmesan, garlic, flour, and the beaten egg in a large bowl, mix, and season with pepper and salt.
5. Next, heat the olive oil in a skillet applying medium-high heat.
6. Use a tablespoon to scoop batter for each cake, put in the oil, and flatten using a spatula.
7. Allow to cook until the underside is richly golden brown, then flip over to the other side and cook.

8. Your delicious Zucchini fritters are ready to be served.

NUTRITIONS: Total Fat: 12.0 g Cholesterol: 101.9 mg Sodium: 728.9 mg Total Carbohydrate: 11.9 g Dietary Fiber: 1.9 g Sugars: 4.6 g Protein: 8.6 g

CUCUMBER SANDWICH BITES

COOKING: 0' PREPARATION: 5' SERVES: 12

INGREDIENTS

- 1 cucumber, sliced
- 8 slices whole wheat bread
- 2 tablespoons cream cheese, soft
- 1 tablespoon chives, chopped
- ¼ cup avocado, peeled, pitted and mashed
- 1 teaspoon mustard
- Salt and black pepper to the taste

DIRECTIONS

1. Spread the mashed avocado on each bread slice, also spread the rest of the ingredients except the cucumber slices. Divide the cucumber slices on the bread slices, cut each slice in thirds, arrange on a platter and serve as an appetizer.

NUTRITIONS: Calories 187 Fat 12.4 g Fiber 2.1 g Carbs 4.5 g Protein 8.2 g

OLIVES AND CHEESE STUFFED TOMATOES

COOKING: 0' PREPARATION: 10' SERVES: 24

INGREDIENTS

- 24 cherry tomatoes, top cut off and insides scooped out
- 2 tablespoons olive oil
- ¼ teaspoon red pepper flakes
- ½ cup feta cheese, crumbled
- 2 tablespoons black olive paste
- ¼ cup mint, torn

DIRECTIONS

1. In a bowl, mix the olives paste with the rest of the ingredients except the cherry tomatoes and whisk well. Stuff the cherry tomatoes with this mix, arrange them all on a platter and serve as an appetizer.

NUTRITIONS: Calories 136 Fat 8.6 g Fiber 4.8 g Carbs 5.6 g Protein 5.1 g

BACON CHEESEBURGER

COOKING: 30' PREPARATION: 10' SERVES: 4

INGREDIENTS

»   1 lb. lean ground beef
»   1/4 cup chopped yellow onion
»   1 clove garlic, minced
»   1 Tbsp. yellow mustard
»   1 Tbsp. Worcestershire sauce
»   1/2 tsp. salt
»   Cooking spray
»   4 ultra-thin slices cheddar cheese, cut into 6 equal-sized rectangular pieces

»   3 pieces of turkey bacon, each cut into 8 evenly-sized rectangular pieces
»   24 dill pickle chips
»   4-6 green leaf
»   lettuce leaves, torn into 24 small square-shaped pieces
»   12 cherry tomatoes, sliced in half

DIRECTIONS
1. Pre-heat oven to 400°F.
2. Combine the garlic, salt, onion, Worcestershire sauce, and beef in a medium-sized bowl, and mix well.
3. Form mixture into 24 small meatballs.
4. Put meatballs onto a foil-lined baking sheet and cook
for 12-15 minutes.

5. Leave oven on.
6. Top every meatball with a piece of cheese, then go back to the oven until cheese melts for about 2 to 3 minutes.
7. Let meatballs cool.
8. To assemble bites: on a toothpick layer a cheese-covered meatball, piece of bacon, piece of lettuce, pickle chip, and a tomato half.

NUTRITIONS: Fat: 14 g Cholesterol: 41 mg Carbohydrates: 30 g Protein: 15 g

PERSONAL PIZZA BISCUIT

COOKING: 15' PREPARATION: 5' SERVES: 1

INGREDIENTS

- 1 sachet fuels Select
- Buttermilk Cheddar Herb Biscuit
- 2 Tbsp cold water
- Cooking spray
- 2 Tbsp no-sugar-added tomato sauce
- 1/4 cup reduced-fat shredded cheese

DIRECTIONS

1. Preheat oven to 350°F.

2. Mix biscuit and water, and spread mixture into a small, circular crust shape onto a greased, foil-lined baking sheet.

3. Bake for 10 minutes.

4. Top with tomato sauce and cheese, and cook till cheese is melted about 5 minutes.

NUTRITIONS: Fats: 3.2 g Cholesterol: 9.8 m Sodium: 10.5 mg Protein: 3.6 g

GRANDMA'S RICE

COOKING: 2H   PREPARATION: 15'   SERVES: 4

INGREDIENTS

- 40g butter
- 1/2 cup brown sugar
- 1/2 cup arborio rice
- 3 cups milk
- 1/2 tbsp ground cinnamon
- 1/8 tbsp ground nutmeg
- 1 tbsp vanilla paste
- 1/2 cup raisins
- 300ml cream

- 1/2 cup brown sugar
- 1/2 cup arborio rice
- 3 cups milk
- 1/2 tbsp ground cinnamon
- 1/8 tbsp ground nutmeg
- 1 tbsp vanilla paste
- 1/2 cup raisins
- 300ml cream

DIRECTIONS

1. Preheat oven to 300F.
2. Grease a 1 liter ability oven-evidence dish
3. Heat butter in a saucepan and add sugar and rice.

4. Stir for 1 minute to thoroughly coat rice.
5. Remove from heat and wish in milk, spices, and vanilla.
6. Stir through raisins then pour into prepared dish.
7. Bake for 30 minutes, then remove from the oven and stir well.
8. Drizzle over cream and return to the oven for an additional hour.
9. Check that rice is cooked through.
10. Return to the oven for 15-30 minutes if required.
11. Serve with extra cream and nutmeg.

NUTRITIONS: Fat: 20 g Protein: 23 g Cholesterol: 25 mg Carbohydrates: 30 g Sodium: 1000 mg

VEGETABLES

GREEN BEANS

COOKING: 13' PREPARATION: 5' SERVES: 4

INGREDIENTS

- 1-pound green beans
- ¾-teaspoon garlic powder
- ¾-teaspoon ground black pepper
- 1 ¼-teaspoon salt
- ½-teaspoon paprika

DIRECTIONS

1. Turn on the fryer, insert the basket, grease with olive oil, close the lid, set the fryer at 400 degrees F and preheat for 5 minutes.
2. Meanwhile, put the beans in a bowl, sprinkle generously with olive oil, sprinkle with garlic powder, black pepper, salt and paprika and stir until well coated.
3. Open the air fryer, add the green beans, close with the lid and cook for 8 minutes until golden and crisp, stirring halfway through the frying process.
4. When the fryer beeps, open the lid, transfer the green beans to a serving plate and serve.

NUTRITIONS: Calories: 45 Carbs: 2 g Fat: 11 g Protein: 4 g Fiber: 3 g

ASPARAGUS AVOCADO SOUP

COOKING: 20' PREPARATION: 10' SERVES: 4

INGREDIENTS

- 1 avocado, peeled, pitted, cubed
- 12 ounces' asparagus
- ½-teaspoon ground black pepper
- 1-teaspoon garlic powder
- 1-teaspoon sea salt
- 2 tablespoons olive oil, divided
- 1/2 of a lemon, juiced
- 2 cups vegetable stock

DIRECTIONS

1. Switch on the air fryer, insert fryer basket, grease it with olive oil, then shut with its lid, set the fryer at 425 degrees F and preheat for 5 minutes.
2. Meanwhile, place asparagus in a shallow dish, drizzle with 1-tablespoon oil, sprinkle with garlic powder, salt, and black pepper and toss until well mixed.
3. Open the fryer, add asparagus in it, close with its lid and cook for 10 minutes until nicely golden and roasted, shaking halfway through the frying.
4. When air fryer beeps, open its lid and transfer asparagus to a food processor.
5. Add remaining ingredients into a food processor and pulse until well combined and smooth.
6. Tip the soup in a saucepan, pour in water if the soup is too thick and heat it over medium-low heat for 5 minutes until thoroughly heated.
7. Ladle soup into bowls and serve.

NUTRITIONS: Calories: 208 Carbs: 2 g Fat: 11 g Protein: 4 g Fiber: 5 g

FENNEL AND ARUGULA SALAD WITH FIG VINAIGRETTE

COOKING: 10' PREPARATION: 15' SERVES: 6

INGREDIENTS

» 5 Ounces of washed and dried arugula
» 1 small fennel bulb, it can be either shaved or tiny sliced.
» 2 tablespoons of extra virgin oil or any cooking oil
» 1 teaspoon of lemon zest
» 1/2 teaspoon of salt
» Pepper (freshly ground)
» Pecorino

DIRECTIONS

1. Mix the arugula and shaved funnel in a serving bowl.
2. On another bowl, mix the olive oil or cooking oil, lemon zest, salt and pepper
3. Shake together until it becomes creamy and smooth.
4. Pour and dress over the salad, tossing gently for it to combine.
5. Peel or shave out some slices of pecorino and put it on top of the salad
6. Serve immediately

NUTRITIONS: Protein: 2.1 g Carbohydrates: 14.3 g Dietary Fiber: 3.4 g Sugars: 9.1 g Fat:9.7 g

MIXED POTATO GRATIN

COOKING: 7-9H PREPARATION: 20' SERVES: 8

INGREDIENTS

- 6 Yukon Gold potatoes, thinly sliced
- 3 sweet potatoes, peeled and thinly sliced
- 2 onions, thinly sliced
- 4 garlic cloves, minced
- 3 tablespoons whole-wheat flour
- 4 cups 2% milk, divided
- 1 1/2 cups Roasted Vegetable Broth
- 3 tablespoons melted butter
- 1 teaspoon dried thyme leaves
- 1 1/2 cups shredded Havarti cheese

DIRECTIONS

1. Grease a 6-quart slow cooker with straight vegetable oil.
2. In the slow cooker, layer the potatoes, onions, and garlic.
3. In a large bowl, mix the flour with 1/2 cup of the milk until well combined.
4. Gradually add the remaining milk, stirring with a wire whisk to avoid lumps.
5. Stir in the vegetable broth, melted butter, and thyme leaves.
6. Pour the milk mixture over the potatoes in the slow cooker and top with the cheese.

7. Cover and cook on low for 7 to 9 hours, or until the
potatoes are tender when pierced with a fork.

NUTRITIONS: Calories: 415 Cal Carbohydrates: 42 g Sugar: 10 g Fiber: 3 g Fat: 22 g Satu- rated Fat: 13 g Protein: 17 g Sodium: 431 mg

HUMMUS

COOKING: 10' PREPARATION: 10' SERVES: 32

INGREDIENTS

» 4 cups of cooked garbanzo beans
» 1 cup of water
» 1 1/2 tablespoons of lemon juice
» 2 teaspoons of ground cumin • 1 1/2 teaspoon of ground coriander.
» 1 teaspoon of finely chopped garlic
» 1/2 teaspoon of salt
» 1/4 teaspoon of fresh ground pepper
» Paprika for garnish.

DIRECTIONS

1. On a food processor, place together the garbanzo beans, lemon juice, water, garlic, salt and pepper and process it until it becomes smooth and creamy.
2. To achieve your desired consistency, add more wa- ter.
3. Then spoon out the hummus in a serving bowl
4. Sprinkle your paprika and serve.

NUTRITIONS: Protein: 0.7 g Carbohydrates: 2.5 g Dietary Fiber: 0.6 g Sugars: 0 g Fat: 1.7 g

MEAT

GRILLED CHICKEN POWER BOWL WITH GREEN GODDESS DRESSING

COOKING: 45'   PREPARATION: 5' SERVES: 4

INGREDIENTS

- 1 1/2 boneless, skinless chicken breasts
- 1/4 tsp. each salt & pepper
- 1 cup rice or cubed kabocha squash
- 1 cup diced zucchini
- 1 cup rice yellow summer squash
- 1 cup rice broccoli
- 8 cherry tomatoes, halved
- 4 radishes, sliced thin
- 1 cup shredded red cabbage
- 1/4 cup hemp or pumpkin seeds
- Green Goddess Dressing
- 1/2 cup low-fat plain Greek yogurt
- 1 cup fresh basil
- 1 clove garlic
- 4 tbsp lemon juice
- 1/4 tsp. each salt & pepper

DIRECTIONS
1. Pre-heat oven to 350°F. Season chicken with salt and
pepper.
2. Roast chicken about 10-12 minutes until it reaches a temperature of 165°F.
3. When done, dismiss from oven and set aside to rest, about 5 minutes.
4. Cut into bite-sized pieces and keep warm.

5. While the chicken rests, steam riced kabocha squash, yellow summer squash, zucchini, and broccoli in a covered microwave-proof bowl about 5 minutes till tender.
6. For the dressing, arrange the ingredients in a blend- er and puree till smooth.
7. To serve, put an equal amount of the riced veggie

mixture into four individual serving bowls.
8. Add an equal amount of cherry tomatoes, radishes, and shredded cabbage to each bowl along with a quarter of the chicken and one tablespoon of seeds.
9. Drizzle dressing on top.

NUTRITIONS: Calories: 300 Cal Protein: 43 g Carbohydrates: 12 g Fat: 10 g

TURKEY CAPRESE MEATLOAF CUPS

COOKING: 45' PREPARATION: 10' SERVES: 6

INGREDIENTS

- 1 large egg
- 2 pounds ground turkey breast
- 3 pieces of sun-dried tomatoes drained and chopped
- 1/4 cup fresh basil leaves, chopped
- 5 ounces low-fat fresh mozzarella, shredded
- 1/2 teaspoon garlic powder
- 1/4 teaspoon salt and 1/2 teaspoon pepper, to taste

DIRECTIONS

1. Preheat oven to 400°F.
2. Beat the egg in a big mixing bowl.
3. Add the remaining ingredients and mix everything with your hands until evenly combined.
4. Spray a 12-cup muffin tin and divide the turkey mixture among the muffin cups, pressing the mix in.
5. Cook in the preheated oven till the turkey is well-cooked for about 25-30 minutes.
6. Chill the meatloaves entirely and store them in a container in the fridge for up to 5 days.

NUTRITIONS: Fats: 14 g Cholesterol: 87.1 g Sodium: 174. 4 g Potassium: 73.9 g Carbohydrates: 1.4 g Protein: 16.9 g

AVOCADO CHICKEN SALAD

COOKING: 10' PREPARATION: 10' SERVES: 2

INGREDIENTS

- 10 oz. diced cooked chicken
- 1/2 cup 2% Plain Greek yogurt
- 3 oz. chopped avocado
- 12 tsp. garlic powder
- 1/4 tsp. salt
- 1/8 tsp. pepper
- 1 tbsp + 1 tsp. lime juice
- 1/4 cup fresh cilantro, chopped

DIRECTIONS

1. Combine all ingredients in a medium-sized bowl.
2. Refrigerate until ready to serve.
3. Cut the chicken salad in half and serve with your favorite greens.

NUTRITIONS: Calories: 242 Fats: 13 g Cholesterol: 44 mg Sodium: 553 mg Potassium: 581 mg Carbohydrates: 18 g

SOUPS AND STEWS

ROASTED TOMATO SOUP

COOKING: 50' PREPARATION: 20' SERVES: 6

INGREDIENTS

- 3 pounds of tomatoes in a halved manner
- 6 garlic(smashed)
- 2 onions (cut)
- 4 teaspoon of cooking oil or virgin oil
- Salt to taste
- Fresh grinded pepper • 1/4 cup of heavy cream(optional)
- Sliced fresh basil leaves for garnish

DIRECTIONS

1. Oven medium heat of about 427f, preheat the oven.
2. In your mixing bowl, mix the halved tomatoes, garlic, olive oil, onions, salt and pepper
3. Spread the tomato mixture on already prepared baking sheet
4. For a process of 20- 28 minutes, roast and stir
5. Then remove it from the oven and the roasted vegetables should now be transferred to a soup pot
6. Stir in the basil leaves
7. Blend in small portions in a blender
8. Serve immediately

NUTRITIONS: Fat: 5.9 g Cholesterol: 0 mg Sodium: 26 mg Potassium: 590.7 mg Carbohydrate: 12.6 g Protein: 2.3 g

CHEESEBURGER SOUP

COOKING: 45' PREPARATION: 15' SERVES: 4

INGREDIENTS

- 1/4 cup of chopped onion
- 1 quantity of 14.5 oz. can diced tomato
- 1 lb. of 90% lean ground beef
- 3/4 cup of chopped celery
- 2 teaspoon of Worcestershire sauce
- 3 cups of low sodium chicken broth
- 1/4 teaspoon of salt
- 1 teaspoon of dried parsley
- 7 cups of baby spinach
- 1/4 teaspoon of ground pepper
- 4 oz. of reduced-fat shredded cheddar cheese

DIRECTIONS

1. Get a large soup pot and cook the beef until it be- comes brown.
2. Add the celery, onion, and sauté until it becomes tender.
3. Remove from the heat and drain excess liquid. Stir in the broth, tomatoes, parsley, Worcestershire sauce, pepper, and salt.
4. Cover with the lid and allow it to simmer on low heat
for about 20 minutes.
5. Add spinach and leave it to cook until it becomes
wilted in about 1-3 minutes.
6. Top each of your servings with 1 ounce of cheese.

NUTRITIONS: Calories: 400 Cal Carbohydrates: 11 g Protein: 44 g Fat: 20 g

MUSHROOM & JALAPEÑO STEW

COOKING: 50' PREPARATION: 20' SERVES: 4

INGREDIENTS

- 2 tsp. olive oil
- 1 cup leeks, chopped
- 1 garlic clove, minced
- 1/2 cup celery stalks, chopped
- 1/2 cup carrots, chopped
- 1 green bell pepper, chopped
- 1 jalapeño pepper, chopped
- 2 1/2 cups mushrooms, sliced
- 1 1/2 cups vegetable stock
- 2 tomatoes, chopped
- 2 thyme sprigs, chopped
- 1 rosemary sprig, chopped
- 2 bay leaves
- 1/2 tsp. salt
- 1/4 tsp. ground black pepper
- 2 tbsp vinegar

DIRECTIONS

1. Set a pot over medium heat and warm oil.

2. Add in garlic and leeks and sauté until soft and translucent.

3. Add in the black pepper, celery, mushrooms, and carrots.

4. Cook as you stir for 12 minutes; stir in a splash of vegetable stock to ensure there is no sticking.

5. Stir in the rest of the ingredients.
6. Set heat to medium; allow to simmer for 25 to 35 minutes or until cooked through.

7. Divide into individual bowls and serve warm.

NUTRITIONS: Calories: 65 Cal Fats: 2.7 g Carbohydrates: 9 g Protein: 2.7 g

SMOOTHIES

AVOCADO KALE SMOOTHIE

COOKING: 5' PREPARATION: 5' SERVES: 3

INGREDIENTS

» 1 cup water
» ½ Seville orange, peeled
» 1 avocado
» 1 cucumber, peeled
» 1 cup kale
» 1 cup ice cubes

DIRECTIONS

1. Toss all your ingredients into your blender then process till smooth and creamy.
2. Serve immediately and enjoy.

NUTRITIONS: Calories: 160 Fat: 13.3g Carbs: 11.6g Protein: 2.4g Fiber: 0g

APPLE KALE CUCUMBER SMOOTHIE

COOKING: 5' PREPARATION: 5' SERVES: 1

INGREDIENTS

- ¾ cup water
- ½ green apple, diced
- ¾ cup kale
- ½ cucumber

DIRECTIONS

1. Toss all your ingredients into your blender then process till smooth and creamy.
2. Serve immediately and enjoy.

NUTRITIONS: Calories: 60 Fat: 3g Carbs: 0.6g Protein: 1.1g

STRAWBERRY MILKSHAKE

COOKING: 5' PREPARATION: 5' SERVES: 2

INGREDIENTS

» 2 cups of Homemade Hempseed Milk
» 1 cup of frozen Strawberries
» Agave Syrup, to taste

DIRECTIONS

1. Prepare and put all ingredients in a blender or a food processor.
2. Blend it well until you reach a smooth consistency.
3. Serve and enjoy your Strawberry Milkshake!
4. Useful Tips
5. If you don't have Homemade Hempseed Milk, you can add Homemade Walnut Milk instead.
6. If you don't have frozen Strawberries, you can use
fresh ones.

NUTRITIONS: Calories: 222 Fat: 4g Carbs: 3g Protein: 6g Fiber: 1g

CACTUS SMOOTHIE

COOKING: 10' PREPARATION: 5' SERVES: 2

INGREDIENTS

- » 1 medium Cactus
- » 2 cups of Homemade Coconut Milk
- » 2 frozen Baby Bananas
- » 1/2 cup of Walnuts
- » 1 Date
- » 2 teaspoons of Hemp Seeds

DIRECTIONS

1. Take the Cactus, remove all pricks, wash it, and cut
into medium pieces.
2. Put all the listed ingredients in a blender or a food processor.
3. Blend it well until you reach a smooth consistency.
4. Serve and enjoy your Cactus Smoothie!
5. Useful Tips
6. If you don't have Homemade Coconut Milk, you can add Homemade Walnut Milk or Homemade Hemp-seed Milk instead.
7. If you don't have frozen Bananas, you can use fresh ones.
8. If you don't have Baby Bananas, add 1 Burro Banana instead.

NUTRITIONS: Calories: 123 Fat: 3g Carbs: 6g Protein: 2.5g Fiber: 0g

DESSERTS

DARK CHOCOLATE MOCHACCINO ICE BOMBS

COOKING: 10' PREPARATION: 5' SERVES: 4

INGREDIENTS

- 1/2 pound cream cheese
- 4 tbsp powdered sweetener
- 2 ounces strong coffee
- 2 tbsp cocoa powder, unsweetened
- 1 ounce cocoa butter, melted
- 2 1/2 ounces dark chocolate, melted

DIRECTIONS

1. Combine cream cheese, sweetener, coffee, and cocoa
powder, in a food processor.
2. Roll 2 tbsp of the mixture and place on a lined tray.
3. Mix the melted cocoa butter and chocolate, and coat
the bombs with it.
4. Freeze for 2 hours.

NUTRITIONS: Calories: 127 Cal Fats: 13g Carbohydrates: 1.4 g Protein: 1.9 g

CHOCOLATE BARK WITH ALMONDS

COOKING: 10' PREPARATION: 5' SERVES: 12

INGREDIENTS

- 1/2 cup toasted almonds, chopped
- 1/2 cup butter
- 10 drops stevia
- 1/4 tsp. salt
- 1/2 cup unsweetened coconut flakes
- 4 ounces dark chocolate

DIRECTIONS

1. Melt together the butter and chocolate, in the micro- wave, for 90 seconds.
2. Remove and stir in stevia.
3. Line a cookie sheet with waxed paper and spread the chocolate evenly.
4. Scatter the almonds on top, coconut flakes, and sprinkle with salt.
5. Refrigerate for one hour.

NUTRITIONS: Calories: 161 Cal Fats: 15.3 g Carbohydrates: 1.9 g Protein: 1.9 g

VANILLA BEAN FRAPPUCCINO

COOKING: 6' PREPARATION: 3' SERVES: 4

INGREDIENTS

- 3 cups unsweetened vanilla almond milk, chilled
- 2 tsp. swerve
- 1 1/2 cups heavy cream, cold
- 1 vanilla bean
- 1/4 tsp. xanthan gum
- Unsweetened chocolate shavings to garnish

DIRECTIONS

1. Combine the almond milk, swerve, heavy cream, vanilla bean, and xanthan gum in the blender, and process on high speed for 1 minute until smooth.
\
2. Pour into tall shake glasses, sprinkle with chocolate shavings, and serve immediately.

NUTRITIONS: Calories: 193 Cal Fats: 14 g Carbohydrates: 6 g Protein: 15 g

SMOOTH PEANUT BUTTER CREAM

COOKING: 0' PREPARATION: 10' SERVES: 8

INGREDIENTS

- 1/4 cup peanut butter
- 4 overripe bananas, chopped
- 1/3 cup cocoa powder
- 1/4 tsp vanilla extract
- 1/8 tsp salt

DIRECTIONS

1. In the blender add all the listed ingredients and blend until smooth.
2. Serve immediately and enjoy.

NUTRITIONS: Calories: 101 Fat: 5 g Carbs: 14 g Sugar: 7 g Protein: 3 g Cholesterol: 0 mg

VANILLA AVOCADO POPSICLES

COOKING: 0' PREPARATION: 20' SERVES: 6

INGREDIENTS

- 2 avocadoes
- 1 tsp vanilla
- 1 cup almond milk
- 1 tsp liquid stevia
- 1/2 cup unsweetened cocoa powder

DIRECTIONS

1. In the blender add all the listed ingredients and blend smoothly.
2. Pour blended mixture into the Popsicle molds and place in the freezer until set.
3. Serve and enjoy.

NUTRITIONS: Calories: 130 Fat: 12 g Carbs: 7 g Sugar: 1 g Protein: 3 g Cholesterol: 0

CHOCOLATE ALMOND BUTTER BROWNIE

COOKING: 16' PREPARATION: 10' SERVES: 4

INGREDIENTS

- 1 cup bananas, overripe
- 1/2 cup almond butter, melted
- 1 scoop protein powder
- 2 tbsp unsweetened cocoa powder

DIRECTIONS

1. Preheat the air fryer to 325 F. Grease air fryer baking pan and set aside.
2. Blend all ingredients in a blender until smooth.
3. Pour batter into the prepared pan and place in the
air fryer basket and cook for 16 minutes.
4. Serve and enjoy.

NUTRITIONS: Calories: 82 Fat: 2 g Carbs: 11 g Sugar: 5 g Protein: 7 g Cholesterol: 16

ALMOND BUTTER FUDGE

COOKING: 10' PREPARATION: 10' SERVES: 18

INGREDIENTS

» 3/4 cup creamy almond butter
» 1 1/2 cups unsweetened chocolate chips

DIRECTIONS

1. Line 8*4-inch pan with parchment paper and set aside.
2. Add chocolate chips and almond butter into the double boiler and cook over medium heat until the chocolate-butter mixture is melted. Stir well.
3. place mixture into the prepared pan and place in the freezer until set.
4. Slice and serve.

NUTRITIONS: Calories: 197 Fat: 16 g Carbs: 7 g Sugar: 1 g Protein: 4 g Cholesterol: 0 mg

www.ingramcontent.com/pod-product-compliance
Lightning Source LLC
Chambersburg PA
CBHW071527080526
44588CB00011B/1585